WHY ARE THE JELLYFISH TAKING OVER?

Jane Walton

JANE WALTON CONSULTING, LLC

Why Are the Jellyfish Taking Over?

Copyright © 2014 Jane Walton Consulting, LLC
All rights reserved. No part of this book may be used or reproduced in any manner whatsoever without written permission of Jane Walton Consulting, LLC.

Written by Jane Walton

Edited by Sarah Gowen

Book design by Floc5

Photography & Illustration Credits

Thinkstock and Annie Robinson

ISBN 978-0-9906136-0-2

First Edition

Acknowledgments:

First and foremost, this book is dedicated to Parke, who provides me with unwavering love and support 24/7. Thank you for cheering me on while I reach for my dreams.

To my marketing and communications team – Sarah Gowen, Sarah Beshears and Melanie Osterhaus – without whom you wouldn't be reading this book.

And finally, I want to dedicate this book to my clients, who want more for themselves and for their organizations, and who allow me to help them explore ways to create balanced, inspiring workplaces.

Why jellyfish?

Jellyfish have been getting a lot of press lately, and not the positive kind. In parts of our oceans, jellyfish populations are growing exponentially, thanks to changes like overfishing and rising temperatures that have tipped their environment out of balance.

If you live near an ocean, or visit the beach often, you may have already seen evidence of this phenomenon close up (hopefully not too close).

You may also have noticed the rising jellyfish population in another, more familiar environment: your office.

Every company starts with an idea, and plenty of passion, optimism and faith. But it doesn't take much to throw a thriving corporate ecosystem out of balance. A rough financial patch, leaders losing touch with their employees, a group in conflict — any of these can lead to an unhealthy workplace where only human jellyfish can thrive.

It's easy to spot human jellyfish if you know what to look for: the once-top performer who now seems disconnected; the executive who no longer speaks up in leadership meetings; the innovator whose work has become safe and routine. When things get off track and the jellyfish begin their takeover, a company's ability to restore balance will be the key to its survival.

When I started my company, my vision was to make the workplace better by provoking thought, conversation and action. The intent of this book is to do just that.

You will be challenged to interpret ideas and fill in the blanks. You will be encouraged to try new approaches, and to see yourself and your workplace through a different lens: the lens of nature.

It is only through balance that you and your organization can succeed. An imbalanced organization can exist (for a while), but it can't thrive. A disconnected employee can endure (for a while), but won't flourish. Imbalance costs companies, families and communities dearly.

I want you to make this material your own, and hope it will inspire you to make better decisions every day – decisions that keep you engaged, balanced and fulfilled.

The alternative? Jellyfish! It's up to you.

For humans, nature provides sustenance, refuge and reprieve.

Nature provides lessons that we can take into the workplace — lessons on what we must do to create thriving organizations with invested, energized workers.

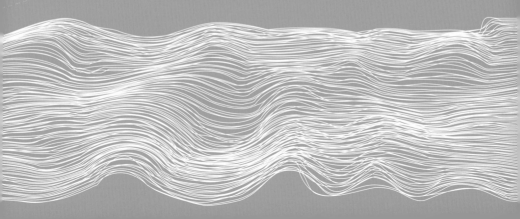

An ecosystem is
a biological community of
interacting organisms
and their physical environment.

An ecosystem includes
living organisms, animals and plants,
and non-living components, soil,
water and air.

When both are in equilibrium,
resources can cycle efficiently—
no group is interrupting the flow
of energy to other parts of
the ecosystem.

LIKEWISE, a workplace is an ecosystem of interacting individuals and their physical environment.

This includes living organisms, individuals and groups, and non-living components, systems and processes, that together create products and services.

When no systemic issues are interrupting the flow of cooperation and progress throughout an organization, efforts cycle efficiently and effectively.

Balance must be maintained in order for an ecosystem to thrive.

When the **balance** of an ecosystem
is disrupted, some species begin to take over
to the detriment of others.

This is happening in our oceans today.

Overfishing and **rising temperatures °**
have led to an explosive growth of
jellyfish populations.

Many creatures cannot survive
these changes to their ecosystem.

But the *jellyfish* are thriving.

Jellyfish

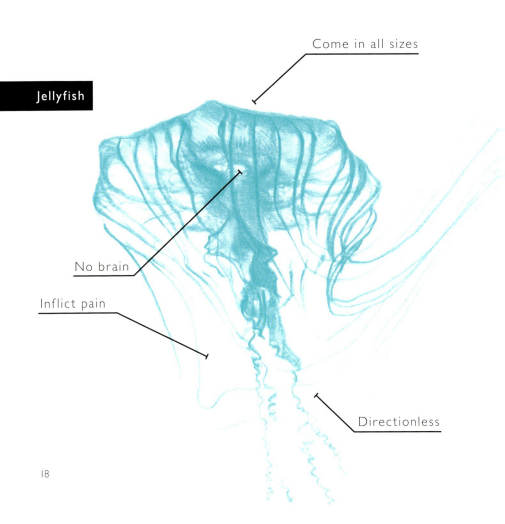

- Come in all sizes
- No brain
- Inflict pain
- Directionless

Are **not strong** swimmers.

Mostly **travel** where the **currents** and tides take them.

Do not have brains or hearts.

Can be as **big** as a human or **smaller** than a grain of rice.

Sometimes **sting**.

Are **found in every ocean** on earth.

In large numbers, have a **negative impact** on the ecosystem.

Jellyfish comes from

the Greek word 'planktos,' meaning

to drift or wander.

There are a lot of parallels between *jellyfish* and burned out, frustrated, disengaged *employees*.

Ever-changing work conditions, lingering fear about job security and lack of confidence in company leadership have led to a dramatic *increase* in the number of people acting like jellyfish.

Innovation and collaboration can't thrive in these conditions.

Human jellyfish

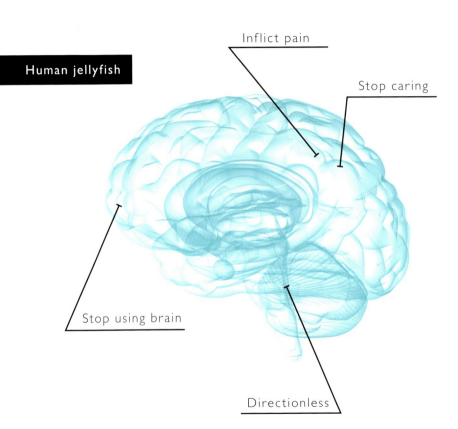

Inflict pain

Stop caring

Stop using brain

Directionless

Go wherever the group takes them.

Stop using their brains and **stop caring**.

Come in **all shapes and sizes**, at **all levels** of an organization.

Can be found **in every organization** on earth.

In large numbers, have a **negative impact** on the work environment.

When human jellyfish begin to multiply in an organization, it is a *symptom* of larger issues.

Issues like:

Short-term focus

Unclear goals and strategies

'Pet' projects that drain resources

Uninvolved employees

Unresolved conflict

Jellyfish at the executive level

When short-term thinking *undermines*
an inspiring l o n g - t e r m vision...

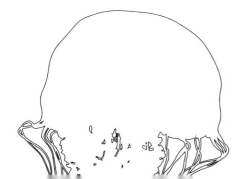

...people will

shift into survival mode and ***stop innovating***.

Without a CLEAR SENSE of the organization's vision, strategies, direction and goals…

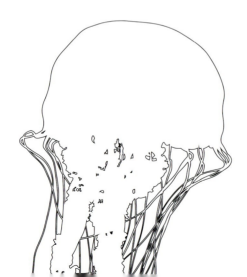

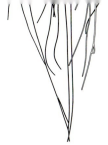

...people will
go wherever the workday takes them.

When **'pet' projects** and initiatives **overload** schedules and

distract from core business functions...

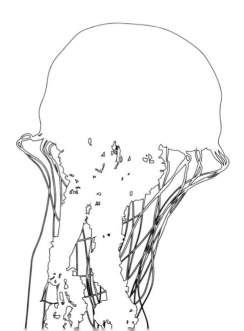

...people will approach the extra *work* with *apathy* and *dread*.

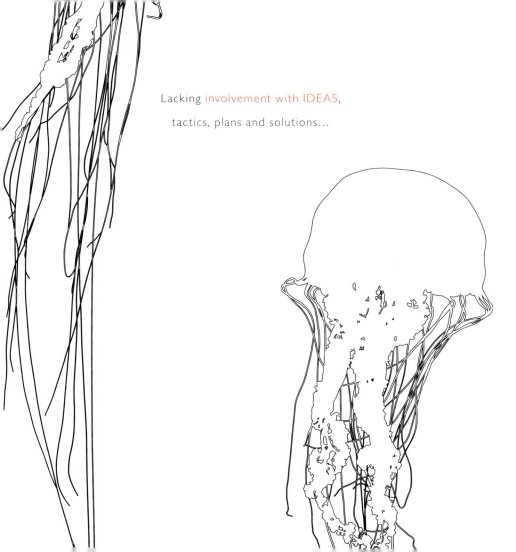
Lacking involvement with IDEAS,

tactics, plans and solutions…

...people will

mindlessly put in their forty hours, week after week.

...people **stop caring** and **learn to tolerate** a dysfunctional workplace.

When human jellyfish reach the organization's HIGHEST LEVELS...

...employees *suffer* – and so does the *profitability* of the organization.

When people feel
DISILLUSIONED, distracted,
discouraged and trapped...

...they cope by turning into *jellyfish*.

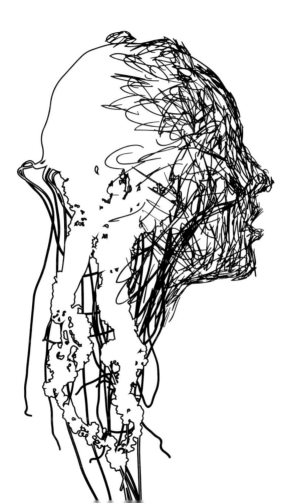

And unless everyone commits
to making a change…

...the jellyfish will take over.

How do we stop this from happening?

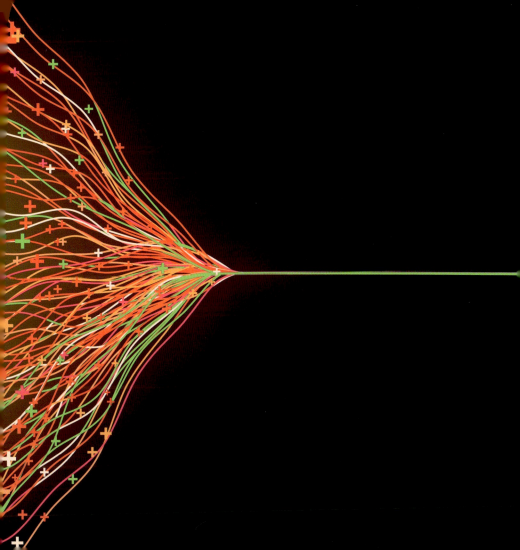

By *regaining* balance.

Balance is the one thing
that can keep the
jellyfish at bay.

Through a balanced workplace,
an organization, and the people
who power it, can thrive.

An evolved approach to creating balance
understands and respects the core needs of

individuals, groups, and the organization,

and meets them in a way that allows
everyone to thrive.

Individuals

In order to thrive, **individuals** need:

A well-suited job

Personal accountability

Willingness to connect and collaborate

Individuals Need

A Well-Suited Job

We all strive to find a job that matches our interests, talents and ambitions — in an organization we can feel proud to call our own.

When we have the skills, knowledge and passion for our jobs, we are likely to succeed.

But when struggle and stress overtake productivity and enthusiasm, it's time to consider whether your job is right for you.

Individuals Need

Personal Accountability

We are all accountable for the work we deliver and how we deliver it.

We each must commit to manage our time effectively and take personal ownership of our work process, outputs and quality.

All of us will make mistakes, and at times feel overwhelmed. When we choose to be accountable — and to ask for help — we can learn and grow, enhancing personal success and satisfaction.

Individuals Need

Connection and Collaboration

When we hold back ideas, honest opinions or enthusiasm from those we work for and with, we create barriers to the success of the team – and by association, our own ability to thrive.

If we instead allow ourselves to connect with others and work cooperatively, sharing both the risks and rewards of teamwork, we can achieve outcomes that benefit our own careers and those of our colleagues.

Groups

In order to thrive, **groups** need:

Clear direction

Timely information

Sufficient support

The chance to be heard

Groups Need

Clear Direction

For groups to thrive, they must know where the organization is going — and the plan for getting there.

All individuals in a group must understand strategies and goals; have a clear focus for their efforts; and have a leader who can keep resources flowing so group members can accomplish their tasks.

Groups Need

Timely Information

Even a team with clear direction can't succeed in a vacuum.

Group leaders must provide continuous communication with employees, letting them know what's happening throughout the organization, how customers are responding, what competitors are doing, and how the group's efforts are contributing to success.

Groups Need

Sufficient Support

Leaders must be closely involved with their groups to understand where and when time, counsel or other support is needed.

The right resources at the right time let group members know that the company is committed to their success, and understands their value to the workplace.

Groups Need

The Chance to Be Heard

Everyone has the right — and the fundamental need — to express their ideas and know that they are heard.

When leaders fail to truly listen to employees' needs and concerns, systems break down and imbalance emerges.

Creating an environment where thoughts are expressed and acknowledged allows information and trust to flow throughout the workplace.

Organizations

In order to thrive, an **organization** needs:

A meaningful vision

Smart business practices

Positive external impact

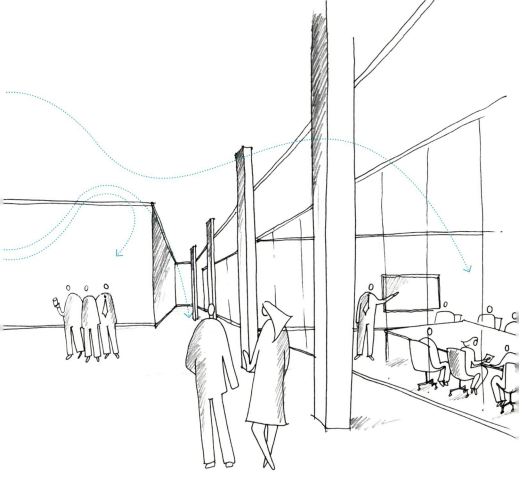

Organizations Need

A Meaningful Vision

At its most elemental level, a vision is about not just surviving, but thriving. While an organization's vision may naturally evolve over time, the initial passion, energy and enthusiasm must remain.

To create and preserve a meaningful vision, we must make sure that it includes the success of all workers, not just a few.

More important still, it must offer everyone a chance to truly contribute to the organization's health, vitality and future.

Organizations Need

Smart Business Practices

In a natural ecosystem, the activities of individuals gravitate toward the most efficient use of energy and resources.

Likewise, business practices must be simple, clear and effective — with roadblocks and non-essential diversions removed — to allow resources to flow properly throughout the entire organization.

Organizations Need

Positive External Impact

As in nature, a company has a ripple effect beyond its own boundaries — specifically, with the customers it serves or otherwise touches.

If our organizations aren't functioning well, neither will the services and products we provide our customers.

When we commit to meeting internal needs first, we can achieve levels of quality, innovation and responsiveness that make a positive impact on our customers and create a sustainable, successful organization.

When these core needs are addressed, employees are focused, engaged and energized. They take personal responsibility for their work and their interactions with others.

Groups feel connected to the organization and to each other. They are supported, informed and contributing to their fullest.

The organization is purposeful and running efficiently and effectively. Individuals, teams and leaders alike feel personally invested in helping the organization succeed – and feel proud when it does.

Through this approach,

- ***trust*** is created
- ***resources*** are shared
- ***innovation*** is supported
- ***collaboration*** becomes automatic
- ***balance*** is restored

and **everyone** thrives.

About the Author

Jane Walton is a leadership and organization dynamics expert who helps companies and their employees work differently – and think differently about work.

Drawing on more than 20 years of experience, Jane approaches organizational issues with the understanding that when people work effectively together the personal and business payoff is substantial.

Described as an executive's lifeline and as the "Obi-Wan Kenobi" of leadership advising, Jane helps leaders simplify and proactively focus their efforts on sustainable long-term success.

An engaging, dynamic public speaker, Jane is able to address serious workplace issues in a direct but positive way.

To learn more about Jane's approach, you can visit janewaltonconsulting.com, which includes an ongoing topical blog.

JANE**WALTON**CONSULTING